the Church is You and I

Confirmation Service and Message

CARL B. RIFE
CAROLYN BISHOP

Lima, Ohio
C.S.S. Publishing Company

I0190313

THE CHURCH IS YOU AND I

0394/ISBN 0-89536-658-4   PRINTED IN U.S.A.

GOD'S PEOPLE GATHER FOR WORSHIP

Organ Prelude and Procession

Call to Worship

Leader: Good morning.
People: Good morning.
Leader: Why have you come here this morning?
People: We have come here because we are God's people and want to worship him.
Leader: And how will you worship him?
People: We will worship him through reading his word, through singing hymns of praise, and through fellowship with others of his people.
Leader: Then let us worship together.

*Hymn

*Prayer for Our Gathering

Our heavenly Father, we gather as your people to thank you that you have promised to be with us always. We're glad you are here in this place this morning as we share in our worship of you and pledge to be a part of your church. Thank you for your love which supports us and for each new day which proclaims your glory and majesty. Amen.

Special Music

GOD'S PEOPLE BRING OFFERINGS

Welcome, Ritual of Friendship and Announcements

Offertory

GOD'S PEOPLE CHOOSE THE CHURCH

Reading: "The Meaning of Our Confirmation"

Today is an important day in the life of the Confirmation Class. Most of us have been in Church School for many years learning about the Bible, the church and Jesus Christ. Since January, we have been meeting together as a class to discuss the meaning of our faith and church membership. We have examined our beliefs about the Bible, the church, Jesus Christ and God and have discovered ways in which we are called to be a follower of Jesus.

We have learned that at our baptism our parents commended us to the care of the church because the church is important to them. At our confirmation today we affirm their choice by saying we choose for ourselves what our parents have shown us is important.

At our baptism, the church chose to accept *us.* Now at our confirmation, *we* are choosing to accept the *church.* Our baptism was a sign of God's acceptance of us. Our confirmation is our acceptance of God and the power of the Holy Spirit within us.

Reading: "Confirmation Is Covenant"

Through our confirmation, we are becoming a part of a group of people with a long history. In the Old Testament God's chosen people, the Hebrews, made covenants or agreements with God. Abraham made a covenant with God. God told him he would be with him on a journey. Abraham did not know where God was leading him, but he trusted God.

The covenant was renewed to the people through Moses. God told Moses that he would lead them back to their own country even though they had lived in Egypt in slavery for many years.

Later on, the prophets reminded the people of their covenant with God. They were unfaithful to God, yet God kept his covenant with them. Let us stand and read together the words of the covenant as recorded by Jeremiah.

The New Covenant

Behold, the days are coming, says the Lord, when I will make a new covenant with the house of Israel and the house of Judah, not like the covenant which I made with their fathers when I took them by the hand to bring them out of the land of Egypt. But this is the covenant which I will make with the house of Israel after those days, says the Lord: I will put my law within them, and I will write it upon their hearts; and I will be their God, and they shall be my people. And no longer shall each man teach his neighbor and each his brother, saying "Know the Lord," for they shall all know me, from the least of them to the greatest, says the Lord; for I will forgive their iniquity, and I will remember their sin no more. (Jeremiah 31:31-32a, 33-34)

Reading and Scriptures

In the New Testament we learn that the church is God's people today. We of the church are chosen to carry on God's work, to tell others the good news that Jesus is alive and will work through us to get his work done. We must constantly search for ways of being God's people in action in the world in which we are living.

Let us hear some Scriptures that speak of the meaning of the church.

"Ye also are built up as a spiritual house to offer up sacrifices acceptable to God by Jesus Christ. You are

4

a chosen generation, a royal priesthood, a holy nation, a PECULIAR PEOPLE." (1 Peter 2:5, 9)

"And he gave some apostles; and some prophets; and some evangelists; and some pastors for the perfecting of the saints, for the work of the ministry, for the edifying of the body of Christ." (Ephesians 4:11-12)

*Affirmation of Faith: "The Korean Creed"

Minister: Where the Spirit of the Lord is, there is the one true Church, apostolic and universal, whose holy faith lets us now declare:

Minister and People: We believe in the one God, maker and ruler of all things, Father of all men, the source of all goodness and beauty, all truth and love.

We believe in Jesus Christ, God manifest in the flesh, our teacher, example, and Redeemer, the Savior of the world.

We believe in the Holy Spirit, God present with us for guidance, for comfort, and for strength.

We believe in the forgiveness of sins, in the life of love and prayer, and in grace equal to every need.

We believe in the Word of God contained in the Old and New Testaments as the sufficient rule both of faith and of practice.

We believe in the Church as the fellowship for worship and for service of all who are united to the living Lord.

We believe in the kingdom of God as the divine rule in human society, and in the brotherhood of man under the fatherhood of God.

We believe in the final triumph of righteousness, and in the life everlasting. Amen.

*Hymn

The Message: "The Church Is You and I"

Special Music

The Ritual of Confirmation

Prayer by Pastor

GOD'S PEOPLE GO OUT TO SERVE

*Hymn

*Benediction

Pastor: Go forth, as sons and daughters of God, knowing that the grace and peace of Jesus Christ is with you.

Confirmation Class: We leave this place, understanding our new responsibility as part of the people of God at our Church.

All: Praise God, Father, Son and Holy Spirit for God's marvelous work among us. We go forth in his name and in his love. Amen.

A MESSAGE FOR CONFIRMATION

The Church Is You and I*

1. The church is people.
2. Not a building.
3. Or a place.

1. Or an organization.
2. But people, like you and me.
3. You and I are the church.

1. We are the church when we are gathered here.
2. We are the church when we are scattered in our community, at home, at school, at work, and at play.
3. When we talk about the church, we are talking about us.

1. When we say, why *doesn't* the church do this or that, we are talking about us.
2. When we say, why *does* the church do this, we are talking about us.
3. Paul said, "You are the body of Christ and individually members of it." The church is a group of people who have a special relationship with each other because of their relationship to Jesus Christ.

1. The church is not a group of like-minded people, but like-hearted people, whose hearts are in Jesus Christ.
2. The church is people who gather for worship, study, and fellowship. The Scriptures say that wherever two or three are gathered in Christ's name, Christ is present and the church is happening.

---

*Intended to be a dialogue between three persons, preferably members of the Confirmation class.

3. The church is people who gather for worship. Worship is the central activity in the life of the church. In worship, we praise God, confess our sin, seek to find his way in our life. We sing, we pray, we listen, we obey. Coming to worship is like recharging our batteries. We are strengthened for the week ahead. Sometimes the strength comes from just hearing the right word in the sermon. Sometimes the strength comes in the quiet times. Sometimes the strength comes from the still, small voice of God which speaks directly to us.

1. The church is people who gather for study. When we come to church, we do not leave our minds at the door. Jesus told us to love God with all our minds, as well as our hearts, souls, and strength. A deep understanding of one's faith goes hand in hand with a whole-hearted commitment to Jesus Christ. A Christian should seek opportunities to explore his faith and ways of putting it into action.

2. The church is people who gather for fellowship. Christians enjoy being with one another. Fellowship is not something we create. It is a gift given to us by God. A Christian needs the warmth of fellowship to keep his faith alive. It is like a live coal. If we remove a live coal from fire, it soon goes out. It needs the other coals to keep it burning.

3. The church is people who scatter to share the good news of God. An alive faith cannot be kept to oneself. It spills over to all areas of life. We do not stop being the church when we leave this building. We are the church wherever we go, sharing the good news that God has sent Jesus.

1. Sharing the good news at home means respecting the rest of your family. It means being helpful around the house, carrying your share of the

responsibilities.

2. Sharing the good news at school means developing your mind and skills to better serve others. It means being truthful and honest in the classroom.

3. Sharing the good news at work means giving an honest day's work for an honest day's pay, treating your fellow workers as you desire to be treated.

1. Sharing the good news in the world means being concerned about what happens to people all over the world — people in the United States caught in the vicious cycle of poverty, people in Africa and Asia dying of starvation, people in other parts of the world, trapped in the middle of violence and terrorism.

All: The church is people.
Not a building.
Or a place.
Or an organization.
But people like you and me.
You and I are the church.

www.ingramcontent.com/pod-product-compliance
Lightning Source LLC
Chambersburg PA
CBHW060045040426
42331CB00032B/2500